WHERE IS JASPER JOHNS?

DEBRA PEARLMAN

Look! Ask a question.
Like a story, a work of art wants to tell you something.
Learning to look carefully can help you understand—
and make looking more fun.
So look! And look again!

PRESTEL

A FLAG OR A PAINTING?

Look at the painting *Flag*.*
Now close your eyes and think of the United States flag.
Can you picture the red and white stripes?
The blue rectangle with white stars?

How is the painting pictured here different from the flag
you imagined?
How is it different from a flag flying outside a building?

The flag stands for the United States of America.
Can it stand for an American?

Look closely at *Flag*.
Are the colors the same as those of the United States flag?
Are there the same number of stripes?
Are there the same number of stars as there are on today's flag?

Jasper Johns was a young artist when he made this painting.
He decided to paint things we have seen many times.
He asked, "Are there things we often see that we
don't really look at?"
Some people asked, "Is it a flag or is it a painting?"

CAN YOU READ THIS PICTURE?

In many of his works, Johns uses a very old method called wax encaustic painting. Famous examples of this type of art are the mummy portraits done in Roman Egypt from about 50 to 300 AD. Colored pigments are added to heated beeswax. It is spread on a surface with a brush or palette knife (like a butter knife only with a wider area to spread with). Imagine melting crayons and spreading the colored wax on paper. Johns began paintings of flags like this one by building up the surfaces with strips of newspaper, which sometimes show through the paint. Can you read letters or words? Jasper Johns likes to hide things and to reveal them. Look at the painting inside the front cover and see what else you can discover.

FLAG, 1954-55

WHAT IS HE AIMING AT?

Ready! Aim! *Wait!* What is Jasper Johns aiming at?
He has borrowed something else we know well,
a target used for practice with a bow and arrow, or a rifle.
Let's use it for "looking practice."
Aim your gaze at the "bull's eye," the smallest circle
in the center of *Target*.
If you stay focused on this "eye," can you also at the
same time see the heads at the top of the painting?

Cover just the target and look at the box with four heads.
Each head is the same, but the eyes are missing. They cannot see.
The mouths are closed. They are not telling us what to think.
What if they could talk? They might say, "Focus on the target.
Start with the blue center and work your way out to the edges:
yellow, blue, yellow, blue, red.
Now you have looked at it carefully."

Is anything peeking out from under the paint?
Use a magnifying glass if you have one. Look for clues!

If we could touch this work, we could change it.
At the top is a lid with hinges. Imagine closing it.
The heads disappear. The target remains.
Ready! Aim! *Focus!*

TARGET WITH FOUR FACES, 1955

WHY RED, YELLOW, AND BLUE?

What colors make the "eye" of *Target*? Red, yellow, and blue are the *primary* pigments used by artists—the colors that cannot be made by mixing other ones. These colors can be mixed to make others: yellow and blue to make green, for example. The American flag is red, white, and blue. If artists had a country of their own, red, yellow, and blue might be their national colors!

WHERE IS HE GOING?

Johns has chosen something else we recognize,
a map showing most of the United States
and parts of Canada and Mexico.
Can you find the state (or province) where you live?
Johns has taken away some jobs we expect a map to do:
it shows no roads or cities.
You couldn't use this map to find your way,
just as you can't fly *Flag* or shoot at *Target*.
Let's try taking away the jobs of the states' names.
Turn the book around so that *Map* is upside-down.

Does this painting have a point to aim at, like *Target*? Or
is it more like a map, letting your eye travel wherever it
wants to go?

Imagine traveling across this map.
Pick the shortest way from South Carolina to California.
Now plan a longer route.
Let your fingers point the way.
Can you see more when you take more time?

MAP, 1961

6

WHERE WAS JASPER JOHNS?

Find Georgia and South Carolina on the map. Johns was born in Augusta, Georgia, and he grew up in a small town in South Carolina. Find the state of New York on the map. Johns traveled north to New York City because he wanted to become an artist and meet other artists. The first real artist he met was Robert Rauschenberg, who is from Texas. He became a good friend. Today Johns lives in Connecticut ("CONN." on the map).

WHAT'S IN THE CAN?

PAINTED BRONZE, 1960

Johns likes to take away the job of an object and give it a new job. The first job of a coffee can is to keep coffee fresh. An artist may use an old coffee can to keep his brushes fresh.

The jobs of this can and brushes are done. Johns has made them into a cast bronze sculpture of paintbrushes in a can. He painted the bronze so that it looks just like the objects it was cast from.

When it is being used, a brush is an extension of an artist's hand, like the hammer of a carpenter or a tennis player's racquet. Imagine grasping each brush's handle, wrapping your fingers around it and pulling it out of the can. Imagine you are Jasper Johns getting started on a new painting. Brush, paint, canvas, and thoughts are ready. There are so many brushes— there are so many possible paintings!

WHAT IS CASTING?

To make a bronze cast of a paintbrush, Johns would first need to make a mould, probably using plaster, of the actual brush. The mould then can be used to create a wax copy of the brush. That copy is covered by wet ceramic "slurry." When this ceramic shell is dry, it is baked in a kiln. This hardens it and causes the wax to melt and run out of the mold. Melted bronze is poured into the hollow shell. When it cools, the shell is broken away, revealing an exact bronze copy of the brush.

FLASHLIGHT I, 1958

CAN YOU SHED SOME LIGHT ON THIS?

Think about what a flashlight is: something to help us look carefully, to find something we could not see. Johns has taken away the flashlight's job and has given it a new one—it is now not something *to see with* but something *to see*. He mounts it on a pedestal, like a trophy or an award, so it seems important. Does this help us pay more attention to it?

Flashlight I (he made others) is covered with an artist's material called Sculp-metal, so that it looks like a sculpture of itself. Is it a flashlight or a sculpture?

9

CAN WORDS HELP YOU SEE?

Look at the words in this painting. Are the painted words like the words you are reading? Can you look through or around them? Do they help you to see the colors they name? Is there a red RED? Is there any yellow in YELLOW? Are all the BLUEs blue? Johns likes to give familiar things new jobs.

The paintings we have already seen have titles that name the things they look like. This is different: the title does not name something we can see in the picture. A periscope is a *way* to see. It can be a tube, with angled mirrors at the bottom and top, that lets you look around walls, corners, or other obstacles. In a submarine, it can let you see above the water's surface.

Look at the half-circle in the upper right. Have you made a snow angel? Or did you ever lie down on a beach, stretch out your arms, and make half-circles in the sand? Who do you think is making this half-circle? Imagine you are in a little submarine that lets you dive among the colors beneath the surface of the painting. You have a periscope that lets you see beyond the painting's edge. If you raise your periscope, which direction would you look, hoping you might see Jasper Johns?

A periscope is like the words in this picture, a way to look through or around something. Jasper Johns is asking you to imagine different ways to look at a picture, so that you can discover more. Remember: Johns likes to hide *and* reveal things. Let's keep looking!

PERISCOPE (HART CRANE), 1967

WHO WAS HART CRANE?

The title of this painting includes the name of the American poet Hart Crane, who lived from 1899 to 1932. Crane used words, as Johns uses paint, to find unusual ways to see familiar things. He begins one of his best-known poems, "To Brooklyn Bridge," by letting us see New York Harbor from the viewpoint of a seagull wheeling out over the Statue of Liberty!

WHICH SIDE IS HE ON?

Imagine slipping out of a pool or bath, leaving wet footprints. Johns made this drawing using his body. Instead of water, he put oil on parts of himself, then pressed his hands to the paper and rolled his head across the surface from side to side.
Do you see his ears?

Johns then sprinkled charcoal onto the paper, and it stuck to the oily parts.
The charcoal shows where Johns has been, like a permanent shadow.

Where is Johns? He looks like he might be pushing through the paper from the other side. Do you think he is hiding?
Or does he seem to be in front of the paper, reaching out to us?

We just saw Johns use his hand instead of a paintbrush. Here he has used more parts of himself to make a kind of print. His body is his "brush," but he has also given his head and hands another job. They have become the subject of this picture, just as the American flag is the subject of *Flag*.

STUDY FOR SKIN I, 1962

RED, YELLOW, BLUE, WHO?

Here is another flashlight: can it help us see?
Remember the periscope that lets us see over or
around obstacles? This flashlight is pointed at a mirror,
a rear view mirror from a motorcycle or a bicycle.
The mirror and flashlight are attached to the front of a
painting, most of whose surface we cannot see.
Imagine the flashlight is on and the mirror is reflecting
its beam of light. Where would the circle of light fall?
On the plate at the lower left?

The plate is attached to the back of a painting, whose
surface is pressed against another painting. We see the
back, not the front of the smaller painting, the part that
is not usually seen. What we usually see is hidden.
Johns is usually hiding, too.

We have met the words RED, YELLOW, and BLUE
several times.

Here they frame a picture of Jasper Johns as a young
man, printed on a souvenir plate—a souvenir being
something we keep to remind us of a place or an
experience. We have found the artist! He is not hiding!
Or is he only sharing with us a memory of himself as a
young man?

Like this painting that faces forward *and* backward,
Johns may be going in two directions: looking back on
his life and work up to this point and forward to what
he will do next.

SOUVENIR 2, 1964

CAN A PICTURE FOOL YOU?

BARNETT NEWMAN, UNTITLED, 1961

A title can be a clue. Johns calls this painting *Ventriloquist*. Ventriloquists entertain people by making a dummy or puppet seem to speak, but it is the ventriloquist who is really speaking. Can an artist fool you by making something painted look real?

Find a nail that seems to cast a shadow. Can you see two heads in profile that seem to be facing each other—or is that a vase? There is a picture here of something that is VERY LARGE in reality. Can you find it?

Johns includes in this painting works by artists he admires. The cups that seem to be floating are by a famous potter, George E. Ohr. The framed print pictured at the upper right is a work by the American artist Barnett Newman.

Compare Johns's painted copy of the Newman print with the reproduction of the actual print on this page. Do you notice anything odd? The Newman print depicted in the painting appears to be reversed: the narrow white stripe is toward the left, not the right. But the flags, even though their colors are unusual, are not reversed.

What if the green flag print were taped to the surface of a large mirror? Would that explain what you see? Perhaps a mirror is a kind of everyday "ventriloquist." Did you know it was a mirror or did Johns fool you? Like a periscope, a mirror is a *way of seeing* that can help us discover new ways of looking at familiar things.

VENTRILOQUIST, 1983

CAN YOU SEE HIM?

Johns was interested in an artist named Edvard Munch (sounds like "moonk"). He lived in Norway and when he was an old man he painted this picture of himself "between the clock and the bed." He is standing upright, like the clock, but we see that he may soon lie down in the bed, where he will rest.

Johns never met Munch in real life, Artists often borrow ideas from other artists. When Johns saw a postcard of Munch's painting, he decided that Munch should be a part of his artistic "family."

BETWEEN THE CLOCK AND THE BED, 1981

18

EDVARD MUNCH, SELF-PORTRAIT: BETWEEN THE CLOCK AND THE BED, 1940-42

In Johns's painting, nothing seems to be standing still!
It is made of three panels, like the three main elements in
Munch's painting: clock, artist, and bed.
Imagine where in Johns's painting these
three elements would be if we could see them.

Compare the quilt or blanket on Munch's bed
to the area in the lower right of Johns's painting.
If you can imagine a person in Johns's painting,
where do you think he might be?

SPRING, 1986

Johns's shadow seems to be "growing" from the boy's shadow. But there is a circular white line that begins at a hand print (remember *Periscope,* p. 11?) and ends in an arrow pointing back to the boy. Are seasons like a circle—always coming around to the beginning? Notice the tree branch above Johns's head. Let's see how it looks in the painting *Summer* on page 23.

This and the following three paintings by Johns are each named for a season of the year. Poets and painters have often used the four seasons to stand in for the "seasons" of a person's life: childhood, youth, maturity, and old age.

In the "family" of artists Johns admires, the Spanish artist Pablo Picasso is especially important. Johns borrowed from two of his paintings for the Seasons series. The shadow was suggested by Picasso's *The Shadow* (at left). As in Johns's painting, the shadow stands in for the artist.

ABOVE: PABLO PICASSO, THE SHADOW, 1953,
RIGHT: PABLO PICASSO, MINOTAUR MOVING HIS HOUSE, 1936

Look at Picasso's picture *Minotaur Moving His House* (at right). What did Johns borrow from it for his picture? Notice the ladder and the rope. Watch for the different ways that Johns uses the ladder in the Seasons pictures.

In Greek mythology, the Minotaur was half man, half bull. It lived in the Labyrinth, a maze designed by Daedalus for King Minos of Crete. Picasso often used the Minotaur as a stand-in for himself.

WHAT TIME IS IT?

How has the tree branch changed? Instead of a blue sky and rain, the stars are surrounded by green. The tree has grown. We can see past Johns's shadow to a wall behind him.

Compare the position of the hand print in the black circle here to its position in the painting *Spring* that you just saw. Is the black disc telling us anything? The arm changes in each painting like the hands of a clock. Look at the painting you just saw and the next two paintings to see if the hand and arm change position.

Look at Johns's shadow. Is he leaning into or away from his work? Is he pushing it or pulling it, like the strong Minotaur? Is the ladder strong too? Can it hold up the big painting by Johns that is suspended from it by the rope?

Besides the half-circle from *Periscope*, do you recognize other clues from Johns's paintings? He is thinking back to his early work. The Seasons are like diaries or memories of his career. He also has added a work by another artist he admires, the *Mona Lisa* by Leonardo da Vinci. Do you recognize her famous smile in Johns's painting?

LEONARDO DA VINCI, MONA LISA, 1503-6

WHAT IS FALLING?

The clock and ladder are splitting Johns's shadow. If you "read" this picture from left to right, the "story" begins and ends with Johns. If he was "growing" within his work in *Spring*, is his work now "falling apart" inside him?

Everything seems to be breaking down. How has the branch from the tree changed with the season? What has happened to the ladder?

FALL, 1986

Do you notice a skull peeking out from the center of the picture under the phrase "CHUTE DE GLACE"? You might see such a sign when travelling in the mountains in France. It means: beware of falling ice. But *glace* can also mean "mirror" in French. Is he warning himself (or us) to beware of mirrors? Of thinking too much about ourselves or the past?

Dots of white paint look like snow falling. The branch from the tree is still above Johns's right shoulder. Can you see it? We can see through Johns's shadow. It is fainter. Is he weaker, too? He was pulling his work in *Summer*. How would you describe the way he is standing now? Does he seem to be leaning? Is he resting? Thinking back on all his work? Or is he getting ready for a new Spring, a new beginning?

WINTER, 1986

HOW FAR CAN YOU SEE?

Here Johns includes a picture of a spiral galaxy deep in space, seen as if through a telescope—another way of looking! This image and some other pictures seem to be taped to a mirror (as in *Ventriloquist*), which reflects still more pictures. Beneath all of them is a plan of the house where Johns's grandmother lived. He drew it from memory.

We find a ladder once more. Here it seems to lead us from the world of Jasper Johns's memories up to the distant galaxy. We remember that the light from a galaxy may take many millions of years to reach our eyes. The stars we see above us are also deep in the past.

Where is Jasper Johns? He has allowed us to see him in many different ways in the paintings and other objects we have looked at. But maybe we should be wary of looking only for reflections of the artist (beware the *glace!*). Perhaps we need to look past the mirror, farther than a reflection of the artist. Now that we have discovered many ways to see Jasper Johns, let's look beyond the mirror's edge. We have only begun to discover his art!

WHO WAS ICARUS?

We may climb and we also may fall. At the middle left, there is an upside-down stick figure, drawn as if by a child, that is borrowed from another painting by Pablo Picasso. This figure represents the boy Icarus. After his father Daedalus (remember him?) made the Labyrinth, King Minos shut him up with his son in a tower so he could tell no one the secret of how the Labyrinth was built. Daedalus was a great inventor and he made wings for himself and his son so they could escape together. But Icarus flew too close to the sun, which melted the wax that held his wings on, and Icarus fell to earth. You recall that Jasper Johns uses wax for many of his paintings. Do you think this myth has a special meaning for him?

MIRROR'S EDGE 2, 1993

ILLUSTRATIONS

All artworks are by Jasper Johns unless otherwise noted.

Front cover and spine:
Target with Four Faces (see page 5)

Back cover: *Souvenir*
(see page 15)

Frontispiece:
Flag above White Collage, 1955. Encaustic and collage (newspaper) on canvas, 19 ¼ x 22 ½ in. (57.2 x 48.9 cm). Kunstmuseum Basel. Gift of the artist in memory of Christian Geelhaar, 1994.
Photograph: Artothek – Hans Hinz.

Page 3:
Flag. 1954–55. Encaustic, oil and collage on fabric mounted on plywood (three panels), 42 ¼ x 60 ⅝ in. (107.3 x 153.8 cm). The Museum of Modern Art, New York. Gift of Philip Johnson in honor of Alfred H. Barr, Jr. Photograph: © 2006. Digital image, The Museum of Modern Art, New York/Scala, Florence.

Page 5:
Target with Four Faces, 1955. Assemblage: encaustic on newspaper and cloth over canvas with objects 26 x 26 in. (66 x 66 cm) surmounted by four tinted plaster faces in wood box with hinged front. Box, closed, 3¾ x 26 x 3½ in. (9.5 x 66 x 8.9 cm). Overall dimensions with box open, 33 ⅝ x 26 x 3 in. (85.3 x 66 x 7.6 cm). The Museum of Modern Art, New York. Gift of Mr. and Mrs. Robert C. Scull. Photograph: © 2006. Digital Image, The Museum of Modern Art, New York/Scala, Florence.

Pages 6–7:
Map, 1961. Oil on canvas, 6 ft. 6 in. x 10 ft. 3⅛ in. (198.2 x 314.7 cm). The Museum of Modern Art, New York. Gift of Mr. and Mrs. Robert C. Scull. Photograph: © 2006. Digital image, The Museum of Modern Art, New York/Scala, Florence.

Page 8:
Painted Bronze, 1960. Oil on bronze, 13 ½ x 8 in. (34.3 x 20.3 cm) diameter. Collection the artist.

Page 9:
Flashlight I, 1958. Sculp-metal on flashlight and wood, 5 ¼ x 9 ⅛ x 3 ⅞ in. (13.3 x 23.2 x 9.8 cm). The Sonnabend Collection. Photograph: Rudolph Burckhardt.

Page 11:
Periscope (Hart Crane), 1977. Oil on canvas, 67 x 48 in. (170.2 x 121.9 cm). Collection the artist.

Page 12–13:
Study for Skin I, 1962. Charcoal on drafting paper, 22 x 34 in. (55.9 x 86.4 cm). Collection the artist. Photograph: Courtesy The Museum of Modern Art, N.Y.

Page 15:
Souvenir 2, 1964. Oil and collage on canvas with objects, 25 ½ x 40 ¼ in. (73 x 53.3 cm). Private Collection.

Page 16:
Barry Moser, Illustration of sperm whale in Herman Melville, *Moby Dick; or, The Whale* (University of California Press, 1981), p. 357.

Barnett Newman, *Untitled*, 1961. Lithograph, printed in black, composition: 22⅞ x 16 5⁄16 in. (58.1 x 41.4 cm). The Museum of Modern Art, New York. Gift of Mr. and Mrs. Barnett Newman in honor of René d'Harnoncourt. Photograph: © 2006. Digital image, The Museum of Modern Art, New York/Scala, Florence.

Page 17:
Ventriloquist, 1983. Encaustic on canvas, 75 x 50 in. (190.5 x 127 cm). The Museum of Fine Arts, Houston. Museum purchase with funds provided by the Agnes Cullen Arnold Endowment Fund.

Page 18:
Edvard Munch, *Self-portrait: Between the Clock and the Bed*. 1940–42. Oil on canvas. 58⅞ x 47 ½ in. (149.2 x 120.6 cm). The Munch Museum, Oslo.

Page 19:
Between the Clock and the Bed, 1981. Encaustic on canvas (three panels), 72 x 126 ½ in. (183.2 x 321). The Museum of Modern Art, New York. Gift of Agnes Gund. Photograph: © 2006. Digital image, The Museum of Modern Art, New York/Scala, Florence.

Page 20:
Spring, 1986. Encaustic on canvas, 75 x 50 in. (190.5 x 127 cm). Robert and Jane Meyerhoff, Phoenix, Maryland.

Page 21:
Pablo Picasso, *The Shadow*, 1953. Oil on canvas, 24 x 19⅓ in. (129.5 x 96.5 cm). Musée Picasso, Paris. Photograph: RMN/© Jean-Gilles Berizzi.

Pablo Picasso, *Minotaur Moving His House*, 1936. Oil on canvas, 18 ⅛ x 21 ⅝ in. (46 x 54.9 cm). Private Collection. Photograph: Orlando photos.

Page 22:
Leonardo da Vinci, *Mona Lisa*. 1503–1506. Oil on wood,. 30 ¼ x 20⅞ in, (77 x 53 cm). Musée du Louvre, Paris.

Page 23:
Summer, 1985. Encaustic on canvas, 75 x 50 in. (190.5 x 127 cm). Philip Johnson Collection.

Page 24:
Fall, 1986. Encaustic on canvas, 75 x 50 in. (190.5 x 127 cm). Collection the artist

Page 25:
Winter, 1986. Encaustic on canvas, 75 x 50 in. (190.5 x 127 cm). Private collection.

Page 27:
Mirror's Edge 2, 1993. Encaustic on canvas, 66 x 44 in. (167.6 x 111.7 cm). Robert and Jane Meyerhoff, Phoenix, Maryland.

Page 29:
Jasper Johns in 1955 at his studio on Pearl Street, in New York City, with *Flag*, 1951–55, and *Target with Plaster Casts*, 1955, in the background. Photograph: George Moffett.

AUTHOR'S NOTE TO PARENTS AND TEACHERS

This book is designed to encourage active, careful looking. Jasper Johns is an artist who has some surprising things to tell us about looking at pictures and thinking about objects. The selection of artworks is arranged chronologically to show Johns's development as an artist and the evolution of his characteristic themes and artistic concerns. However, individual works can be studied separately, or several works may be compared. Johns's work is layered with meanings, but these may be understood differently by different viewers—or even by the same viewer in a different frame of mind. Thus the book will reward repeated readings, looking and looking again, and asking fresh questions—deepening a young reader's engagement with the work of Jasper Johns and with the world of art.